ALLOW LOVE TO BE

PRAISE FOR REBECCA'S WORK

"Rebecca's work is profoundly and powerfully transformative and is unlike others because hers is rooted in limitless, boundless love. Other teachers want and need identity and that's perfectly fine, but I love that she yields to love over personal identity for your own boundless growth and joy and that of others, and you can quote me on that. I'd have to have daily therapy for 1000 years to uncover and unravel the things I have uncovered and unraveled so quickly while working with Rebecca. Even then, even if I had a thousand years my mind couldn't have seen what my awareness knows. That old sadness is now restored to Love and the clarity that I am whole is restored as well. I love this so much!"

- Kathleen M., Tucson Az.

"My prior 40 years of seeking pale in comparison to the true understanding I have relaxed into after working with Rebecca.

In previous studies, love was mentioned and even emphasized, but was never transmitted in its fullness the way that I have experienced with her."

- B.D., NY

"Rebecca's work transforms everything for me now. I was intense seeker for truth for last 7 years, but there always was feeling like all this seeking is like job, a constant battle. I tried tons of techniques (I think more than 23 different ones). And this is miraculous! Now I feel tons of love coming out of me and everything just transforms inside of me without doing and everything is just like play. Can't wait to continue in the next series!"

- Dainius, Lithuania

"Rebecca offers the highest truth in the most accessible way. She always keeps things light, easy, and real. While working with her, it feels to me like a bridge is built between my highest understanding and my current perception. This has allowed me to deepen my experience of a peace and love beyond description, while at the same time witnessing changes in my life that I could have previously only wished for. To name just a few: a far greater natural appreciation of myself, smoother and happier relationships, feeling at home in my body and life, and generally living a life that is punctuated by miracles, rather than blanketed by a nondescript "stuckness" that I had felt before working with her."

- L.R.

"I describe Rebecca's work as (truly) integrating the mind, body and spirit. About six weeks in, I said to her "wow, I forgot to worry." My seemingly natural set-point of worry and disapproval was disappearing! Her work is gentle, thoughtful, methodical – and the most profound that I have found."

- Jan, CA

"Rebecca creates such a safe space within which to 'emerge'. She has no judgment. Things that looked to me like 'the end of my world' she was able to put into the perspective of love, and 'poof' it was suddenly a non-issue! I was truly blessed to have had her as a mentor. Thanks Rebecca!"

- Jenny La Fontaine, Intuitive Messenger

Additional experiences can be found at:

www.RebeccaQuave.com/what-others-say

Allow Love to Be

Rebecca Quave

You Are Not Broken

You Are What
You Have Been Looking For

Love is All There Is

CONTENTS

PREFACE

This book is compiled from teleconference sessions. As you read it, take your time to interact with it as if you were there in the moment.

Undertake the introductions and conclusions of the sessions as meditations. Read them slowly and allow yourself time to experience what arises in you.

Read the sections with callers as though you are each caller. Allow the topics to connect with what they mean for you.

Take time to absorb the content and allow yourself to curiously explore the space that's being offered.

Let yourself connect with what is alive in the words and more importantly, in the spaces between the words.

All you need is already within you.

This is an opportunity to point your attention back to the changeless Truth within, and rediscover the Love you Are.

Because these sessions are from live interaction, you will find much of the tone is casual and conversational.

Kindly forgive any transcription errors and colloquial expression, and let yourself connect with the underlying Truth as you read.

Some edits have been made for simplification and clarity. Any identifying information has been removed.

Session 1: Truth

Introduction:

Truth as a Priority

Take a moment to settle in.

Bring your attention out of whatever you've been doing before now.

Bring your attention back from whatever you are anticipating happening later today or tomorrow.

Just have a nice deep breath, and allow that to be important enough to take up your whole attention.

Let your very existence be important enough to take up your entire attention.

Allow exactly what you are experiencing right now to be enough to get your whole attention, whatever that may be… even if you think you are experiencing something unpleasant.

Can you allow yourself to be with your breath, and just be with whatever is there?

Everything you are experiencing is just as sacred as everything you are looking to experience, that you are hoping to experience, that your mind has gotten the idea is better somehow.

Stay with a nice deep breath, all the way through your body, all the way down through your feet.

Allow yourself to pay attention to exactly what you are experiencing.

I know it sounds incredibly simple but it is really the most important thing you can do.

How I can support you really depends on what you are really looking for, what is most important to you. The best way I can support you is if what you are really looking for, if what's most important to you, is Truth.

That's because as far as I can see, one of the biggest lies that you've been sold and that you've sold to yourselves, is the pursuit of trying to manipulate your surface level, conscious experience into just one side of duality.

What I mean by that is, thinking your goal is to feel what your mind calls 'good and happy and positive' all the time.

Many people have the idea of a linear spectrum, with everything you call 'bad and negative and things I don't want to feel' on one end and everything that you call 'happy and good and what you want to feel' at the other end.

Then you think your job is to move your little slider from wherever you are now all the way over to what you call 'the good end' and just keep it there.

And if that's what you are attempting to do, it's always going to end in frustration. It's always going to end in frustration because your surface level experience is constantly in flux, it's constantly changing.

If what you are trying to do is rooted in separation, then you think you have all kinds of bad junk you have collected and need to get rid of.

If you think when you are experiencing anger or sadness that what you need to do is to get rid of it, that's going to result in frustration.

There will be times when, at a surface level, you think you succeed in doing that, but then you will also feel, 'well now it came back', 'now I feel it again'.

Instead, what you need is a total inclusion. What you are doing is a complete integration, an all-embracing, all-inclusive, total integration of everything that is You.

Even when you hear me talk about the part of you that's already completely peaceful, that already exists and you are just not paying attention to it, your job isn't to somehow get to that peaceful place and try to separate from everything else.

It's a total inclusion.

It's you letting all of that exist together as it already does, which will mean you are rooted consciously in a peaceful, changeless place and at the same time allowing everything you experience to unfold.

Now, where this gets a little funny for the mind is once that does happen, even the surface experience does tend to shift back into harmony.

And anytime there is a disharmony it restores itself to harmony very quickly. But the mind tends to jump to the mistaken conclusion that this happens by separating things out and removing them.

I'm giving you a reminder of where we are working from. We are not working from, "Hey everybody, do some cartwheels to get yourself happy again!" because then what? Do you just do more cartwheels all the time?

What I am addressing is the totality of you. The totality of you, not just that surface level experience.

As you know, you could go around distracting yourself and doing every positive trick and tip and waving your magic wand left and right, and if you have underneath it all an unaddressed sense of despair, or agony, or separation, or a boiling rage that's been hidden and suppressed, you will have to run from it forever.

If you are here now, I think you don't want to do that. If you are on this call, then what you are interested in is the absolute Truth of the totality of you, which turns out to be Love - not love in the way that word has been used, but Love which has no bounds and no opposite.

The purpose of this call is to come together in a vortex of Love and to move forward in Truth.

BRINGING PRESENCE TO LIFE TRANSITIONS

Caller 1:

I handed in my resignation for my job because things got totally out of hand. I had the boss and others treat me like I was a completely aggressive person.

It was just really bizarre because I wasn't feeling that way at all. I guess now what I question is why I had to go through it, when I went into it with the total desire to be complete love. Now I have to find a new job.

But throughout it all, I think I stayed feeling loving and that is a complete miracle. The whole situation just doesn't really make sense to me.

Rebecca:

That's fantastic.

So let's deal with what's here now, because the reason I open the lines as much as possible is to walk you through the practical moment-to-moment process for you, rather than just speaking to you from my perspective. You would like it and it would feel true to you, but there could be a gap afterwards where you wonder, "Ok but that's not how I feel, so now what do I do?"

The most important aspect of this is staying with your direct experience.

Can you love your adorable mind? It's very helpful for a lot of things, calculations, you name it. Can you appreciate that it's looking to help you out, trying to puzzle out what's going on, trying to work out why it's going on, trying to fix it?

Can you just give it a big hug and let it know, "You did your best on this and it's ok"?

Now, just stay with your direct experience, whether you even have words to describe it or not.

Nice big breath.

Just feel into all the things you just described to me. Just see what shows up about that: whatever confusion, whatever dissatisfaction, whatever anxiety, whatever, you name it.

Just notice it showing up, notice the experience in your body.

Give it your full attention right now. Include all of it; allow all of it.

Now you can go ahead and invite up the root of this.

There's something this situation has activated for you that is not new.

There's a root of something that was left unexperienced at the time, was left unresolved at the time, and now has been waiting for you to fully experience it.

Usually when it shows up to be experienced you think something's wrong. But then it has to wait until next time.

So, invite it up. Let yourself know you can handle it, you are willing to experience it right now.

Love doesn't mean everything being perfect in duality. Love means allowing it to Be.

Love means that it has permission to exist exactly as it Is.

That goes for you and that goes for all your experiences and your feelings.

What do you notice?

Caller 1:

I'm having a feeling of excitement of how I, you're right, I've had experiences like this and I let them devastate me and this time I actually said to myself at one point, this must be something I had to go through just to see that I don't have to become devastated, that I can take charge.

Rebecca:

Exactly. So, invite that forward, that whole part of you that believed for so long that you were devastate-able, that in certain situations you would be rendered powerless.

Invite it into the space.

Remember, it's not about getting rid of that part because it is wrong, it's about letting it exist within the totality of the Love you are.

When you let it exist in the totality, what actually happens is the tendency to identify with it completely dissipates. Your tendency to identify with it has been a result of your resistance to it. Resistance throws you into identification with it.

Do you see that now?

Caller 1:

Yes, I do.

Rebecca:

You are infinite.

If you are infinite there is no getting rid of anything. Good luck with that. Where would you put it? (Laughter) You go on forever. So keep looking for where your trash chute is, so you can throw something out.

What you *can* do is let it all come into harmony because you are consciously including it, because you are not imposing all these imaginary separations.

How does it feel now?

Caller 1:

It feels good. Because before I took the job I really thought I wanted to do something different because I've had bad experiences in it and now that I gave my notice, I'm feeling, for the first time, much more confident to pursue something in a new field.

Rebecca:

Put everything in terms of what's pulling you forward.

So even when you say, 'I am moving on from that field,' rather than it being because you had bad experiences from it, as that implies you have to run from that.

How about, "I am moving on from it because it's not for me anymore"? "I am moving on from it because there is something new for me to do."

Caller 1:

I actually said those very words to my daughter. I can't believe you are saying it.

Rebecca:

There you go. Now you get to hear back that you are 100% on the right track with that.

Caller 1:

Yes, wonderful confirmation.

Rebecca:

As a reminder, stay with the direct experience.

Whatever is happening, that's the most important thing you can do. Bring your attention to the direct experience, raw, exactly as it is, and you'll notice it always unravels itself.

The mind has gotten the idea there is so much more you need to do, that there's some kind of process and trick and manipulation you have to do, because that's the context that it works in.

When you stay present with your direct experience, you immediately have access to what you already Are. It just comes rushing through where you thought it wasn't there. That imaginary, imposed separation falls and everything harmonizes.

I'm only holding that door in you open for you to connect with you. And then we go from there.

INTEGRATION AND SELF SABOTAGE

Caller 2:

I worked with the other caller which was really good for me because before getting on the call I was feeling very disconnected, I was feeling exactly the way you described the linear line and wanting to move from real feelings of despair and grief and confusion right into the happy place and looking for that magic wand and I know there is no such thing.

I know that is a fantasy and a fairy tale. I would love to integrate.

Rebecca:

Let's do that. There is such a thing as a magic wand, but you Are it.

I want us to really dig into that tendency you mentioned, of trying to make the move across the spectrum (or up the spectrum) from bad to good.

Take a nice deep breath.

Give yourself permission to start to notice and recognize the part of you that already exists in one step more than the best place you can imagine.

If you think it is bliss, let yourself connect to one step past that.

If you think it is peace, let yourself connect even with one step past that.

Go to whatever is one step more than what your mind even has a word for.

Now from here, bring in front of you all the things you thought are on the bad end of the spectrum, all the things you think you don't want to experience.

What's the worst thing that can happen, being the infinite being you are, if you let yourself experience those in this moment?

The grief, the sadness and depression - the reason those experiences have endured, have lingered, is your war with them, your fight with them, your judgment that they are wrong and bad and you are trying to get quickly out of them and into something else.

You've tried to be separate from them, when in reality, those experiences are in you.

Let your attention widen out so you are not strictly in that very pin-pointed place of identification where one experience is your whole experience.

Allow it to be there.

Stay with the direct, raw experience of it.

Let yourself feel how and where it shows up in your body. Stay present with it.

Invite all of it, all the way back to its root to come out into the open to be embraced, included, integrated.

Include everywhere that what you are experiencing now is only part of what it is that has been un-acknowledged, unresolved, unexperienced, and all the things you thought that means about you.

Right now there is a really big fear of you being that person. There is a really big fear of you being nothing but grief, a big fear of you being locked in depression.

Caller 2:

Yeah.

Rebecca:

What if the only question is whether or not you are going to fight with that?

Caller 2:

I don't want to fight with it, I want to integrate it and allow it to reveal...

Rebecca:

It's ok, you don't need to fight with it.

So let the very root of it come out into the open, into this embrace.

Give it permission to exist exactly as it is.

Give yourself permission to experience it exactly as it is.

That's what you loving you is.

It's that you can experience anything at any moment, while still being embraced in Love.

Loving yourself doesn't mean you do all sorts of shenanigans and gymnastics to force yourself only to what you think is the happy end of the scale.

Most people are using self-love as a tool and a manipulation to try to move themselves to one side of duality. That's never really going to work because it's not what Love is.

Caller 2:

It's actually harmonizing on its own now.

Rebecca:

Exactly. Stay with it. Keep breathing with it.

Nature always teaches us everything. All the time.

If you look into nature, everything isn't all green, or all brown, or all anything. Not every plant blooms at the same time of year.

Nature doesn't have its perfection by trying to push itself all to one end of duality. There's everything on the spectrum happening all at the same time, all in perfect harmony.

And that's what's possible within you; that's what's natural within you.

Caller 2:

Including the withering, the dying off.

Rebecca:

Exactly.

You can't move from changing to changeless - they aren't separate.

You allow yourself to be rooted in the changeless part of you, while allowing the level that is constantly changing to be constantly changing.

You can't impose your true changelessness on the level of reality that is always only changing.

You can't impose the absolute, unspeakable Peace and stillness onto the level of your experience that is made up of a continuous flux of experience and emotion.

I see many people beating their heads against the wall trying to do that, and taking their own self love down the gutter in the process.

Invite out into the open any residual expectation you had on yourself about maintaining the thing you have tasted in meditation.

Look at the belief which says you are doing it right if that's what you're feeling all the time at your surface level of experience.

Caller 2:

Exactly. I am a victim of that. I am such a victim of that. You are definitely reading the energy here.

Rebecca:

So, invite that up.

Can you let yourself off the hook for that whole expectation?

Can you let yourself instead start to experience the continuity of what you were dipping into, and experience that it is always there even if you are in the midst of the biggest tantrum of your life?

Caller 2:

Yeah.

Rebecca:

There you go, let that all just melt together.

The mind, bless it, does the best it can to make sense of all this. It gets to observe you experiencing the truth of what you are and it says, "Oh my, let's have that all the time!"

But Truth is already here all the time.

On the surface there's still whatever: broken dishes, people we love passing on, and celebrations, and everything in between.

Caller 2:

The mind also likes to sabotage it too. At least my mind sometimes says, no no no, can't let you go there.

Rebecca:

Tell me what you mean by sabotage?

From my perspective we are inherently not as self destructive as we've gotten a reputation for.

So tell me what you mean by sabotage and let's see if that's what it is or if there's another explanation.

Caller 2:

Resistance, perhaps is the other explanation. This resistance to allowing all there is to be.

Rebecca:

That's not sabotage.

That's just what the mind is set up to do.

The mind is not set up as an allowing mechanism. The mind is set up as a doing mechanism.

If you pull out your calculator, you can sit there with it forever and it's never going to show across the top of the calculator screen some new and original bit of poetry, is it? Never. But it's one hundred percent reliable for what it does. You put in numbers, it calculates, it gives you a new number, right? That's it.

Does a calculator sabotage poetry? No. it just doesn't have the capacity for poetry.

Start examining these beliefs because you could get into judgment and polarity about it and suddenly be at war with even your own mind.

So, what if it was never sabotaging you? What if there are certain things within its realm and certain things that aren't?

Caller 2:

Yes, that's much more reasonable.

Rebecca:

Can you Love it for what it does do and Love it for what it doesn't do?

Caller 2:

Yes, I can.

Rebecca:

That's it. There you go. Ok?

Caller 2:

Yes, beautiful. Thank you.

Rebecca:

Keep going with that, stay present with whatever is showing up.

Moving Beyond Resistance

Caller 3:

I experienced an amazing family reunion and then I decided to see if I could experience even better than that and so I had Thanksgiving which had temper tantrums and yet all this wonderful love and everything like that.

It was quite an amazing thing. I like what the person was saying before because I was thinking I sabotaged and caused the temper tantrums.

Now I realize that I can just experience the temper tantrums and they can also be wonderful too. They can expand out and allow people to bloom. Does that make any sense?

Rebecca:

It makes sense.

The only part of you that is afraid of temper tantrums, that resists temper tantrums, is the part that is believing a lie - the part of you that believes you are something far more limited than you are.

The Truth of you has no reason to care that a temper tantrum shows up in its experience any more than the whole sky cares when there's a storm somewhere.

Caller 3:

But it feels like the sky is falling in when you have a temper tantrum, when somebody is doing...

Rebecca:

It does feel that way when our identification is shrunken down to just where the temper tantrum is.

When identification is placed wholeheartedly in our constructed self, it can be threatened by something like that.

That limited constructed self can be threatened by our own temper tantrum, by somebody else's temper tantrum, or whatever. So, if that's where your identification is, it's very scary, of course. Then you are under threat, you are in danger, or you are the one spewing off, which puts you under another type of threat as you could get thrown out of the tribe for acting like a lunatic and being a danger.

Caller 3:

You know, that's amazing because what had happened was I just left the room and walked off. I was in a separate room and I was just looking out the window, and I said, what am I doing? I am an infinite being, why am I so afraid that I am going to be tossed out the window about this thing? I did go back to it though.

Rebecca:

That's good. Even though you gave yourself that space, what you want to do is feel the fear, stay present with "Oh no, they are going to throw me out the window!"

You said, "Well I am an infinite being so there's no reason for me to feel that."

Well, you are an infinite being so you are totally allowed to feel that. It's not going to hurt you to feel that.

Take a deep breath right now.

Let it come up, the whole resistance, the fear of being under threat, everything that has always, in the past, come with your reaction to somebody spewing off - whether it's somebody else or you having the tantrum.

Caller 3:

Yes, it was also me wanting to throw them out the window but not wanting to admit that.

Rebecca:

There you go.

So all the judgment of that, all the avoidance of that, all the trying to separate from it, go ahead and let yourself feel it right now.

The whole totality of it.

Never mind out a window, how about off a cliff?

Caller 3:

Well, I am on third floor so it's...

Rebecca:

Ok, out a window is a pretty solid deal then. Go ahead.

Caller 3:

It's harmonizing out.

Rebecca:

All you have to do is be with it.

That's all you have to do.

It's so simple.

It's right under our noses and it's exactly what we don't do.

Caller 3:

Right, because I ran from it instead because I believe I'm not supposed to feel that way.

Rebecca:

Yes, because we have bigger and better ideas of how sparkly we can be! Meanwhile we already Are, oh my goodness, if we could just get that. We already Are and what amplifies it is the willingness to include, the willingness to integrate, the willingness to embrace, every single thing. Every single thing.

So, bring something else.

What's another thing you usually try to use all your tricks on? Where do you think, "I'm not supposed to feel this, I am more evolved now, yadda, yadda, yadda…so I'll do a thing and get to feel a different way."

What's the number one thing you do that to?

Caller 3:

Ha ha ha! My number one love affair with avoiding something like that would be with money.

Rebecca:

Ok, so money isn't really a raw feeling or experience. Money is a concept.

Caller 3:

It feels like it though.

Rebecca:

Yes, it feels like it. That's what I want to get to.

Whenever you think of money, what is the raw experience of it and not the mental gyrations about it?

So when you say money, what happens in your body? Where do you feel it?

What do you feel?

Caller 3:

All over. It just immediately goes from the head to the toes of just dread.

Rebecca:

Take a nice deep breath and let yourself experience that.

Experience the total dread, head to toes dread.

Stay with it.

Let yourself feel you are one hundred percent under threat from every angle.

Caller 3:

Oh my goodness, yes.

Rebecca:

Your mind is on duty to try to find you a way out of it, but that doesn't let you resolve it.

So stay present with it.

Go ahead and feel it.

What is it like to be in total head to toe dread?

Caller 3:

Wow. This is awful.

Rebecca:

It's well within your infinite capability to feel totally awful.

Caller 3:

Oh, but I don't like feeling totally awful.

Rebecca:

Why? Because you think you are so limited that's all you are if you feel it?

Caller 3:

Ah, yes, not supposed to do that.

Rebecca:

Well, it's not about supposed to.

Remember, if your priority is to feel nice, that's fine, but my priority with you is Truth, total Truth, the unshakeable Truth of what you Are.

Caller 3:

I didn't realize that that's what I had bound myself up with.

Rebecca:

Keep breathing.

Stay with letting that experience roll through your body. That total dread, it's like a trapped animal with nowhere to run. It's really intense.

Caller 3:

It's very intense. Yes.

Rebecca:

Make sure you are actually breathing.

Because otherwise one of your body's possible reactions is to just seize up, shut the whole thing down and just die before anything gets to you. Ok?

Caller 3:

(Laughter)...

Rebecca:

And that's what you are anticipating and that's why you freak out and try to get away from it. So just stay with it.

Caller 3:

There's lots of this dread. It's like, big.

Rebecca:

Yes, invite up the bigness of it.

Invite it up all the way from the root, all the way from every time you've experienced it.

Go to the root of the feeling of being absolutely under threat, completely trapped, no way out, that causes that total dread in the body.

Caller 3:

Oh yeah, because now that you've said that, I can go back and I can see where they've trained all of us to have this dread. My father, my grandfather, on all sides, yes.

Rebecca:

Ok, so let the whole root of it come through you now.

Caller 3:

It's harmonizing.

Rebecca:

Shockingly enough, everybody keeps saying the same thing, "Oh, it just harmonizes." Yes, it does.

So keep letting it harmonize.

It's going to do its own thing.

Stay present with it.

Let it roll through.

Caller 3:

It's like shining a flashlight in a dark room.

Rebecca:

Yes, it sure is.

You don't have to wrangle all that darkness into a trash bag and throw it out, do you?

Caller 3:

No, but I have been working hard at doing that now that you mention it.

Rebecca:

I know sweetheart, so many people have. (Laughter) Because the more trash bags you wrangle up and throw out, the more you are going to slide across that scale of duality into the good bit, or up that scale of duality into the good bit, and stay there, right?

Caller 3:

There goes my job description. Nice, very nice.

Rebecca:

Except I know what's really been your job description all along, and you are already doing it.

Caller 3:

Now that all this wrapping darkness things up into garbage bags is taken off the list, nice.

Rebecca:

Now just feel into where you're at when I say, money.

Caller 3:

It's like, just a word. It's just a word, that's it.

Rebecca:

What if you could actually feel great about it?

That will show up on its own. I don't want you to try to force that as all of this finishes unraveling.

Now you have enough clarity to look back and see what's been happening:

The dread you just dealt with, anytime there was a whiff of it, your mind could smell that dread coming from a hundred paces, right?

And it would say "Oh no!" And it would launch itself into action: "I'm going to do this to get some money, I am going to do that to get some money," and so on, all to keep the dread at bay.

Meanwhile, the dread just needs your total attention and will wait for it.

Do you see how many times you turned it away?

Caller 3:

Yes, I was just talking about that this morning that I do that. It's amazing.

Rebecca:

Yes, well everybody does. So that's why the key to this is absolute simplicity.

You can bring your mind into a big hug and let it settle down until that pressure is off of it while you stay with the direct experience of the feeling.

Caller 3:

That's amazing because how many garbage bags have I taken out about money? Ha ha ha!

Rebecca:

Well, you've tried to take it out.

You are infinite, so show me where you put them that isn't still in you.

Caller 3:

Oh, I hadn't thought about that. They have to go somewhere don't they?

Rebecca:

I think so. And they are going to smell eventually.

Caller 3:

(Laughter) Ok. I am going to let all of those guys harmonize and do their thing. All the bags I have taken out.

Rebecca:

All of it. That's all you can do.

Caller 3:

That clears out a lot of stuff. It just clears out space.

Rebecca:

Yes! It's truly all that you have to do.

Caller 3:

Wow. Thank you.

Be All-Embracing

Rebecca:

Generally you've gotten habituated into doing the opposite of simple embracing.

Those of you who have been exploring spirituality for ages, which is most of you, then you get habituated upon habituated. You get habituated into all the tricks and gymnastics that are meant to undo what you think was your conditioning. But then that's conditioning on conditioning.

There's no way out through the same mechanism. Code doesn't unwrite code. More code doesn't undo code.

You've got to go back a step. Most of what's happening when people are pursuing self expansion, and spirituality, is they are now seeing the difference between what shows up on a computer screen versus the source code. And they are trying to use the source code to rewrite the source code.

Instead, you have to go back another step. Only the person writing the code can change it.

The mind doesn't have the capacity to change its own structure.

It can be harmonized, just not from itself.

Take a nice deep breath.

Allow yourself to feel the fullness of that support that's available to you.

There's nothing wrong with you.

There's not some big thing you need to overcome or some big block that you have or any of that.

It's as simple as knowing what's really going on and knowing how to address it at the level that it can actually be addressed, knowing how to deal with it directly at the level it can actually be harmonized.

And from there, it's going to seem to the mind so incredibly simple. And it really is. That's what makes it more powerful than anything that the mind can whip up.

Invite up all judgments you had on things that serve different functions, different purposes, and you've put them in a hierarchy, you've ranked them as one is better than another.

Let that fall away.

Let yourself see it for what it really is.

Let yourself see the different areas of function that each serve what they serve.

Let each aspect of your experience be what it is.

They don't have to be ranked in a hierarchy. You are much more than that.

Have you had the attitude that a situation in your life is something really bad that you need to get out of, or something that is really bad that needs to be fixed?

Have you tried to duke it out on that level of duality with the mind or have you sat down and gotten really present to your direct raw experience about it?

Stay completely present with it.

Keep breathing.

Notice how and where it shows up in your body and just stay with it.

Notice what happens as you give yourself permission to experience it exactly as it is.

Whatever that response is, whatever the reaction is, just experience it, without putting any judgment or expectation on it.

Just breathe and allow it to be.

Resolving Overwhelm

Caller 4:

I'm struggling with the feeling of separation. It has gotten intense.

I feel like the possibilities are crashing, kind of monumentally. So some things are moving through and some aren't and I am kind of mixed up.

Rebecca:

Nice deep breath.

Are you ready to let yourself experience everything you have been holding back?

Caller 4:

Yes.

Rebecca:

Gentle deep breath.

Just stay present with it.

Let your attention be fully on the experience itself.

Let your attention be with how that energy is coming through, how and where you are feeling it, noticing it in your body.

Everywhere you did not want to fall apart - allow that to go ahead and unfold now.

Just stay present with it.

Give yourself permission to feel what falling apart feels like.

Invite up the whole root of what has been ignored, unacknowledged, unresolved, avoided, resisted… just invite it to come out into the open.

Allow yourself to experience it now.

What do you notice?

Caller 4:

An easing of the emotions, a freeing of it.

Rebecca:

And what did you have to do to make that happen?

Caller 4:

(Laughter) Nothing.

Rebecca:

Right.

But it did need your attention.

It needed your direct attention instead of your mind running off, bless it, trying to find ways to fix it.

Caller 4:

True, yes.

Rebecca:

If there is one thing you can hear today and really take in, it's to let your mind off the hook from believing there is anything it can do or even anything it should do to fix, or undo or change your experience.

Now part of what the mind hears when I say that is, "Oh no! We'll have to sit in the mud forever."

Let's acknowledge that.

That's not what it means.

It means the mind is off the hook because that's not the way these things get resolved.

Nothing gets resolved by the mind running off to fix it or the mind coming back with a bunch of cockamamie tools for you to do on yourself and trick yourself into being somehow better.

It's just a band-aid. There's nothing wrong with a band-aid, but it's not going to set a broken bone either.

Nice deep breath.

Just pay attention to how much energy is spent with your mind in overdrive to try to come up with solutions.

Can you go ahead and be present to that?

Go ahead and embrace it.

What do you notice?

Caller 4:

Quieter. An ability to breathe easier.

Rebecca:

And that's crucial. There's nothing your mind can go run around doing that is going to resolve anything when you can't even breathe. How effective do you think you are in that kind of state?

Caller 4:

Not effective.

Rebecca:

Exactly.

But here's how this divides into two paths.

Your mind hears that and thinks, "I'm not effective in that state so we've got to make sure I never go into that state."

But even in that state where you are totally ineffective and you are not breathing, the key is not to reject it.

The way out of it is to let yourself be completely present with it and let yourself experience it.

It's not a way out of it, it's a way through it.

Focus on the truth of inclusion and all-embracing oneness. It's what harmonizes in a way the mind is not built for.

Now when you think about your general situation, what do you notice?

Caller 4:

(Giggles) I don't see an answer yet but I don't feel like it is going to stay this way. It feels Ok. It feels welcoming.

Rebecca:

And it's fine to not know things. The mind makes a distinction based on whether it thinks you are under threat or not. You might not know which thing in your fridge you're eating for lunch tomorrow but is your mind worked up about that? Your mind is not worked up about that because it doesn't think that is a threat.

Let's take it to the root.

Invite forth everything that comes with the reactions in your body when your mind has judged something as a threat.

What happens when your mind thinks you are under threat, your identity is under threat, your happiness is under threat, your survival is under threat?

Sometimes people get the most reactive when their power feels like it's under threat, their being right feels like its under threat, right?

Caller 4:

Right.

Rebecca:

So, just let it have the space to come up and just keep breathing.

Let it all move through, let it all shake out and do whatever it needs to do.

Stay present with it.

What happens?

Caller 4:

It's lightening.

Rebecca:

Yes, it gets lighter and your darling mind didn't have to do a thing did it?

Caller 4:

Nope

Rebecca:

Can you keep applying that, moment to moment, as best you can?

Caller 4:

Yes

Rebecca:

Wonderful. Thank you.

Conclusion

It is really so simple.

Nice big breath.

Just allow Truth and harmony to prevail. Go for Truth first.

Find out that what arises from Truth is Love.

It's not love in the way you've ever defined it before.

It's not love that is set up in duality as the opposite of hate. It is Love beyond measure and without opposite.

Have a deep breath, and just let Love expand.

Let it move out from you, and let yourself notice when the echo comes enveloping you back.

Allow the echo of all you are gifting out right now to hit your heart, amplified more than you could have possibly imagined.

Let the echo of this tremendous amplified Love that has been sent out as a gift over the whole planet come back to your own being, come back into your own heart - a million times over, a billion times over, infinitely expanded.

Feel that echo hit back to your own heart.

Let yourself be refreshed, revived, reminded of the truth of you.

Pay attention again to what you really are.

You are so beautiful. I thank you so much for being you all the time, but for also joining here together today. I greatly appreciate it when you embrace your own truth, embrace your own Love. There's nothing sweeter.

Session 2: Love

INTRODUCTION: LOVE AND REJECTION

Take a nice deep breath.

Have a few intentionally full breaths.

After that, give your mind permission to sit back and just observe your breath.

Allow the breath to be exactly as it is, whatever that may be.

Let yourself watch and notice it.

Is it very full? Is it staggered? Is it even?

Does it have the space to circulate through your whole body?

Give your mind permission to observe that, without trying to alter it in any way.

Just watch what's actually there.

Give your breath permission to settle into its own natural rhythm.

Give your body permission to relax into receiving all that is brought with your breath.

Invite out into the open whatever you're experiencing right now.

Check to see what expectation you have about what you should experience, what you need to experience.

In that judgement, in that expectation, check to see what you are rejecting in order to have that expectation.

If you think you should be something else or you think your experience should be something else, other than what it is, then there's a rejection of what you are now, or of what you think you're experiencing now.

So invite out in to the open now the energy that's spent on that rejection.

Notice the amount of effort it takes to reject any part of you, to reject any part of your experience, and ultimately, to reject the unconditional Love that's looking to come pouring through you all the time.

It's always available to you; it's what you Are.

Love is at the core of everything. Then on top of it, all the things you think you are rejecting, those are all just covers, just fronts, for rejecting that Love.

Check and see, all the things you are rejecting, you'll notice the reason you think you're rejecting them is because you think they are other than Love.

You think if you're being that or experiencing that, then you won't have the same access to Love, then you'll be less loved, less lovable - because those traits or those circumstances are somehow separate from Love.

Invite out into the open everything that's been blamed for what you think is your lack of Love, when actually you are turning away from Love and rejecting it.

Maybe you've rejected something about your body or state of health because you think it being that way somehow gives you less access to Love.

Maybe you've rejected a financial situation or circumstance with the belief that it makes you less lovable, that it restricts your access to the unconditional Love you Are.

Maybe you've blamed a conflict you have with another person or what looks like a disharmonious relationship, maybe you've rejected it because you blame it, because you think it restricts your access to Love.

But what if you always have the exact same access to the Love you Are, and the only thing that restricts it or seems to dampen it, is you turning away from it in order to reject the things you think restrict you from it?

What if right where you are, just as you are, without moving an inch or fixing a thing, you could be willing in this moment to give yourself permission to start to notice how tremendously you're being embraced right now?

What if you were willing, right in this moment, to give attention to the massive unconditional Love that's surging through you right now?

It's ready, it's available, it's looking to both pour through you and embrace you from all sides.

Take a nice deep breath

Let's start there, because we can't deal with anything else without coming through Love.

Love is the gateway for everything, so if you're looking away from it, that has to be resolved first.

You must be willing to let it come through you, and embrace you, and let yourself Be it.

Feeling Unloved

Caller 1:

I'm feeling so much calmer just from the first few minutes of the call, and a little bit teary now because I'm feeling the Love coming in. It's just what I needed. Maybe I should just let it continue.

I was feeling confusion before, to do with my work situation. I've been offered a new position a few times before, but I wasn't interested. Now I was offered the position again and I wondered if I should take it but I do have some fear about it. I think I shouldn't let fear stop me and I should accept it. Now I've been in the position a few weeks and some old patterns have been coming up. So I thought this is for me to choose a new way of being, but it's very taxing though.

Rebecca:

Let's look into it.

First of all, nice deep breath.

The Love you said was starting to come through, just have a nice deep breath and give yourself permission to soften to that Love.

As it starts to pour through, you just become softer and softer and allow it to permeate you.

Caller 1:

It's like walls are coming down.

Rebecca:

Exactly - that's all it takes.

All that Love does is Love.

So it Loves even the walls, even the rigidity, even the old patterns. It Loves all of that.

So you don't have to find a way to destroy those to let Love through. If you just let Love through, it just Loves them into itself.

Then they are Love again as well. So they don't have to be destroyed. They are just met with Love and become Love again.

Which to the mind looks like they were destroyed, but it's not something the mind understands.

All it takes is that willingness that says, "Yes, I'll cooperate with that, I'll yield to Love, I'll soften to it, I'll let Love do its thing."

Do you notice how much that's moving now?

Caller 1:

Yes.

Rebecca:

Good.

So now from there, let's bring your whole work situation into this place. Let's let it come meet you here in Love.

And really what's under that, it's not about a work thing, it's about a you thing, isn't it?

Caller 1:

Yes. From birth, just a pattern that's been repeating because I didn't feel loved.

Rebecca:

Everything you thought was a pattern that's caused you problems, go ahead and invite up all the wrongness and judgement that's been there about the pattern.

Your mind thought the judgment and making wrong of it was helping you, because to your mind that was a step forward from letting the pattern run totally unseen.

Thank your mind for being willing to take a step to recognize that pattern and bring it out in the open and say "aha, you're the troublemaker."

But what if instead of calling the pattern a troublemaker, you just recognize it as what thought there was no Love and needed more Love?

So even the pattern itself that you've been battling, would you invite it up and give it permission to be surrounded and embraced in the Love it thought it was missing?

Caller 1:

Yes.

Rebecca:

Because that whole pattern and belief was built on believing Love isn't present or accessible.

So then when you judge even that pattern as wrong or bad, it only breeds more of it. It continues in a circle, doesn't it?

Caller 1:

Yes.

It feels so good to be letting the Love in.

Rebecca:

That's what you can carry forward through the whole situation. Let yourself recognize the pattern, but rather than judge it or make it your enemy, be glad that the pattern got your attention so you can now offer it the Love it thought wasn't there.

Caller 1:

Yes, thank you.

Rebecca:

You're welcome - thank you for speaking up.

Loving What You Don't Like

Caller 2:

I noticed that I get very stubborn and jittery inside when I try to allow Love in the presence of all kinds of things I think are not ok.

Rebecca:

Yes, that's just internal alarms going off to signify your belief is that those things are separate from Love.

Caller 2:

Yes, they are very hard-headed.

Rebecca:

They are very protective of you is all.

Caller 2:

(chuckles) Well I don't really love them.

Rebecca:

That's ok - you don't have to because Love Loves them already anyway.

Did you ever have a day as a child when you knew you would be comfortable without a jacket but a parent was determined to get you to wear a jacket? Did you ever know that you felt the right temperature to go out and then felt burdened if you had to carry around a jacket you didn't need to wear?

But what was the parent or grandparent's intention? It wasn't to burden you, was it? It was to protect you, right?

Caller 2:

Yes, to protect me.

(chuckles)

And I know because I've also been stubborn with trying to do this to my own children.

Rebecca:

Can you give stubbornness permission to be embraced by Love?

Caller 2:

Yes.

Rebecca:

Take a look at stubbornness, determination, perseverance, tenacity, and everything you've judged as good or bad along that continuum of different versions of that energy.

Can you allow the whole continuum to collapse and be embraced in Love?

Caller 2:

Yes, it gets softer.

Rebecca:

In that softness, invite all the protection mechanisms that are setting off all those alarms to come out into the open and be Loved exactly as they are.

Caller 2:

Yes,

Rebecca:

Check again to see if you can give permission for Love to move through everything.

Caller 2:

Yes,

Rebecca:

Then when Love meets any resistance or hesitation, would it be ok if Love remains there Loving the resistance and hesitation?

Caller 2:

Yes,

Rebecca:

What's happening internally is, something is getting your attention and when you fully give it your attention it can resolve.

Caller 2:

Sometimes it seems there are so many things like that.

Rebecca:

That's ok, take them one by one.

And it won't always seem like so many because as you continually give your attention then there's no longer a backlog of things waiting.

Caller 2:

Yes, thank you. I see that. I'll stay present with each one.

SELF-LOVE AND SELF-SABOTAGE

Caller 3:

I really resonated with every word of the opening of the call. I would like some support with just loving me.

There seems to be a pattern of a lot of self-sabotage. I've done a lot of work on it, but I feel like I can't get past where I am now. So I'm frustrated and rejecting it.

Rebecca:

I'm glad you spoke up about it.

What we tend to call self-sabotage, I don't see it as that, because you don't really ever work against yourself.

You may do things that look that way, but it's only things crying out for Love and attention.

It's never really to take yourself down.

Invite out into the open all the effort and work you've put into trying to love yourself, and give permission for the whole thing to just fall away, while thanking your mind for its valiant effort.

The truth is that's not a project for the mind to undertake and you don't need to expect the mind to even understand how to Love you, much less succeed in doing it.

Because in reality you already Love you.

You already Love you so immensely you couldn't describe it if you tried.

Love already Loves you more than your mind could ever hope to try to imitate.

Would you be willing to start to open to that and allow it to come through you?

Caller 3:

Yes

Rebecca:

Whenever Love shows up to do what Love does, are you willing to just answer, "Yes"?

Are you willing to just allow Love to Love?

Caller 3:

Yes

Rebecca:

Which includes you, doesn't it?

Caller 3:

Yes

Rebecca:

So all the work, all the effort, all the striving, and the judgement, expectation, and perception of sabotage … let it all come out into the open.

Let it all be met with the truth.

Let it be met with the Love that's already there, that's already embracing you, and is ready to come pouring through you.

And it doesn't need you to 'like' everything about yourself first for it to happen.

Because of the mind's mistaken definition of love, it limits love to "that's my favorite" or "that's the best."

When your mind sets out to make you Love yourself, then it becomes a constant scorecard of trying to get everything about yourself to be your favorite before you can have Love for yourself.

Do you see how conditional that is?

Caller 3:

Yes, I often feel unworthy of love.

Rebecca:

In reality, Love already Loves you.

You can't even try to describe how immense the Love is for yourself, and it's not waiting for anything about you to change.

It's not waiting for anything you could do or be to earn it.

You can Love something you may not think you like about yourself.

You can see it for what it is, which doesn't for a moment stop Love from Loving it.

That's why it has felt like so much work for you to Love yourself. Because the mind's understanding of loving yourself is to continuously convince yourself that everything about you is the way you think it's supposed to be, until you reach the pinnacle of that effort, and then you win and finally have the option to love yourself.

Caller 3:

Wow, yes.

Rebecca:

Start playing with what it feels like to take the items on your unworthiness list, dive into them, and state whatever it is and then include after it: … and I'm in Love, … and I'm embraced by Love … and Love pours through me anyway.

For example:

"Someone told me at 5 years old I was bad… and I'm in Love …and I'm embraced by Love… and Love pours through me anyway."

Really feel the sting of the judgement against yourself, then dive in and open up to really feel Love wash through you.

Play around that way with everything you think needs to change.

Even if something does need to come into greater harmony, it's Love that supports the blooming of that.

It can't be judged into improvement.

And make no mistake, Love also inspires and supports action when action is required.

Love gives a peace and a power and a freedom of movement to do what is most helpful in any situation.

The mind often has a misconception that you must choose between Love or action, but there is no either-or.

Love is what gives rise to the most powerful movement or action.

Caller 3:

Thank you very much.

Rebecca:

Thank you.

CONCLUSION

Take a nice deep breath.

Let yourself have a few deep breaths all the way through your feet.

Give permission to the Love without opposite, the Love without condition, the Love beyond measure or description, to move through you.

Let yourself start to soften and let yourself open up to allow that Love to come bubbling up through you.

Watch it start to fill the space at the very center of you, filling it so full it has to spill over.

Watch it overflow into more of yourself.

Let it start to saturate everything it comes into contact with, filling it up completely...

and because it's full, spilling over,

so as it flows out and fills up your whole system,

as it expands, it is never diluted or weakened.

Let it move like honey - filling up and then spilling over, filling up and overflowing, because there's more and more of it bubbling up.

Let it wash through every part of you that felt empty.

Let it smooth over everything that felt raw or frazzled, coating it like a balm.

Let it seep into everything that felt hardened or rigid.

Watch how it moves; notice it's never in any hurry.

When it meets a place that seems blocked in you, it doesn't rush to break that door down. It just meets it and starts filling whatever space is there, until that starts to give way to more space it can fill, that it can saturate, until it's so full it starts to spill over.

Only once your whole system, your whole body, your whole being, feels that if you don't let this spill over from you that you'd just burst,

only then, let it start to overflow from you.

As you allow it to expand, notice that allowing it to expand out from you doesn't deplete it.

It's just overflowing, just spreading out because there's more and more of it.

Let it run through you completely.

Allow Love to flow through you and let it be amplified by allowing it to expand through everything and everyone that ever felt separate from Love.

Allow Love to Be.

Session 3: Presence

Introduction:
Practicing Presence

Take a moment to settle in.

Give yourself the space to let yourself have your entire attention.

Take a moment to set aside this time for yourself.

Create a moment which is for you, to get in touch with you, to explore you.

Create a moment in which you give yourself the space to be open to receive.

In this space, give your attention to your own experience, whatever it is in this moment.

Whatever you sensations are physically,

whatever your thoughts are,

whatever waves of emotions you notice ...

Let yourself give everything about your current experience your full attention.

Let yourself observe it.

You can feel and notice your breath as it moves through your body.

Just watch your breath, without trying to make it be anything in particular.

Notice that if you can observe your breath, if you can just experience it directly, if you can let yourself sink into feeling what the breath feels like as it moves through the body, then you can bring the same level of observing and experiencing to anything and everything.

You can bring it to whatever is in your experience right now.

If you have any physical discomfort, you can let yourself just feel it, the same way you feel your breath moving through your body.

Just observe it the way you observe your breath moving through your body.

If it seems you have a runaway train of thoughts and mental activity right now, then the same way you can give your breath your full attention and observation, without trying to make it be or not be anything in particular, you can do the same thing with the mental activity and thoughts.

Without trying to make it be or not be anything in particular, just see what the experience is of having those thoughts and watching those thoughts.

If you're feeling lots of emotion right now, the same way you feel your breath moving through your body and give it your full attention to observe it, you can do the same with any feelings. Instead of trying to make them be or not be anything in particular, or trying to make them stay or go away, just find out what it is to feel them, to fully experience them and observe them.

In the midst of all of whatever needs your attention, let yourself notice that behind all of it your breath is still there, so you can always bring your attention to your breath simultaneously with whatever else you're noticing and observing.

Let yourself start to settle into a sense of ease with that.

Let yourself open up even more.

Step back from judgment about anything you're experiencing or not experiencing.

Let some of your attention fall into what is changeless - into what is untouched by any thought, what is unchanged by any emotion, what is changeless through any physical sensation.

Let yourself open up to the stillness, the quiet, the changelessness, which all you can observe arises from and returns to.

There's no need to stop any feeling or sensation from arising.

Trying to stop things has created your predicament in the first place.

You feel something and try to stop it; so it doesn't get to finish.

If you didn't interfere in any way, everything would reach its conclusion.

Everything that arose would naturally return to the changelessness it came from.

Let yourself have a few nice, deep, gentle breaths.

There's lots of change underway now.

Many people are under recommendation to stay home.

My recommendation to you has always been to "stay at home," but not in terms of your physical dwelling, but to stay at home in what is the home of you and the Truth of you, to remember who you are and let your point of identification rest in that truth - to let your point of identification rest in that changelessness and stillness even as anything you do happens.

That's still my recommendation.

All the things you may be experiencing now provide you even more opportunity to recognize the importance and value and utility of having your point of identification in the Truth of you.

That's what you always have. No matter where you are - in your house, out of your house. No matter what seems to be going on, what you always have is you and what you always have is whether or not your identification is resting in Truth or not.

Any suffering you've ever experienced is because your point of identification was not resting in Truth and so you didn't feel at home in yourself.

Even though it's always there for you because you've never left - you're always there.

It's always there and it's always available.

The Peace which comes from your point of identification residing in Truth is the real happiness, the greatest happiness.

It's a Peace which is unshaken by anything.

That's what's available to you because it's what you Are.

Allowing All Feelings

Caller 1:

Hi Rebecca! I'm so happy to be here with you!

Rebecca:

It's mutual, as always.

Caller 1:

What going on for me is I'm super excited to be stuck at home. Because it's bringing me a sense of being more grounded in the Truth of who I am and what I can offer that's uniquely me.

It's also brought me into witnessing all the things I have used as distractions to be busy and do things the way other people do them rather than just coming from that place within myself (like you said) that's always there and is always right and True.

I'm also feeling all the feelings and energy moving and all the things people are dealing with, and it stirs up stuff in me as well. And I'm finding this time is valuable for me to just sit with it, and it just moves. Like you said, it just moves.

Rebecca:

Yes, it does on its own.

If you don't distract yourself from anything, you experience it all.

We are conditioned that we have certain feelings we don't want to experience, but they are pushing and trying to come across our attention so then they can be complete.

So when you're willing to let all of it be experienced, then all you have to do for the rest of eternity is watch this incredible tapestry unfold.

Caller 1:

Yeah, I think it's more beautiful than I can even imagine.

Rebecca:

It is.

Do you feel that percolating up from inside your heart right now?

Caller 1:

Yeah, I do.

Rebecca:

Just let that expand and spread out.

Caller 1:

(Laughing, then quiet pause)

It's so beautiful.

Rebecca:

Yeah, so you feel the shift that happened?

There was a little residue that things come up but they need to be "dealt with."

They felt "deal-able" and not overwhelming to you, but there was still a little assumption of opposition there, right?

Caller 1:

Yeah, thank you.

Exploring Peace and Love

Caller 2:

I just wanted to ask if you could help with going from this place of peace into a place of love.

Rebecca:

Of course.

To be clear, when I use the word Love, I don't mean the emotion love, which has an opposite.

I mean Love as an energy which has no opposite. It's an all-embracing, all-encompassing field.

It is present within the Peace, it's part of it, and it's a gateway to Peace.

When we are looking from separation and duality, when we're not all-embracing and allowing of everything and allowing Love to do what it does, then we don't feel peaceful.

So it's the movement of Love which allows us to settle into Peace.

Take a nice deep breath.

Let anything come to your attention which you've had any disturbance or judgement about.

Caller 2:

Ok

Rebecca:

Because of the nature of the Love I'm referring to, we can't expect the mind or ego (which are based in duality) to know how to "do" Love. The mind works in opposites and polarities.

Let yourself step back a moment and just watch Love itself start moving through whatever you had disturbance, judgement, or uncertainly about.

Step back and instead of asking the mind to Love it, just let Love itself Love it.

And if the mind wants a job, the mind can maintain a sense of curiosity, which says something like, "I wonder if Love Loves this…"

The mind can have its ideas or judgements about it, while it then wonders, "I wonder if Love Loves this…"

What do you start to notice?

Caller 2:

Well, I am in that space which I wanted to be in.

The space of perfect, all-encompassing Love, without any traces of duality. Thank you.

Rebecca:

Now that you notice being completely in that Love, the mind can be tempted to think there's something it needs to do to maintain it, and it tries to do that from a place of separation. It expects to need to remove anything which seems the opposite in order to not interrupt this experience.

In reality, the opposite is true.

In reality, that Love is like a fire which consumes whatever you throw on it and actually burns higher. Just like when you throw wood on a fire and the fire consumes it and the wood becomes fire, in the same way Love isn't inhibited by anything which seems to be its opposite.

So now from this place of all-encompassing Love, invite in anything which ever seemed like it could interrupt this or give you the opposite feeling.

Invite it all into the center of this, to be completely consumed in Love, for Love to totally embrace it.

Caller 2:

Well everything I tried, it all just drops like a drop into an ocean.

Rebecca:

Beautiful. Thank you for bringing this to everyone.

Caller 2:

Thank you so much.

Resisting Stillness

Caller 3:

I have problems being at peace with things that don't run the way I want them to.

I got organized and prepared for personal distancing. I wanted to write a cookbook and paint, and I'm on my own now. The only thing I do is go for walks and cook, but instead of having time to to the things I wanted I have to keep going to the dentist to get a repair on my braces.

It's hard to be at peace about all that.

Rebecca:

Let's get in touch with the part of you which resists stillness.

There's a part of you, which for whatever reason, doesn't want to be still, or is even maybe afraid of Peace.

Invite that part of you out into the open, even if you haven't been aware of it before.

Open up and as that comes in front of you, check and see if it feels separate from Love. And check to see if Love itself already embraces it.

Allow yourself to step back and observe, watching Love itself embrace everything in you that holds any resistance.

Watch Love permeate anywhere in you that's afraid of Peace or uncomfortable with Peace.

Caller 3:

Yeah, it makes me sad.

Rebecca:

Let the sadness arise and let yourself experience the sadness directly.

Follow the sadness all the way back to its source.

There's something there in you before the sadness arose, which is the same when the sadness is there, and continues to be the same after the sadness is gone.

Follow the sadness back to that, back to is own source.

What is the stillness the sadness arises from and returns to?

Caller 3:

I feel like I can't get in contact with that.

Rebecca:

That's ok.

Can you check to see if Love itself Loves the sadness?

Can you step back and allow Love to Love the sadness?

Caller 3:

Yes, I can do that.

Rebecca:

Do you see that the sadness itself was behind the resistance to stillness? Because if you were still enough then the sadness was going to have space to arise.

Caller 3:

Yes, and other things as well -

"Stillness is boring" and things like that.

Rebecca:

There's a tension created when you say you want stillness but other things are interrupting it, when meanwhile the interruptions are happening because you're actually internally conflicted about it.

Going forward, be really gentle with yourself.

Let go of any expectation about what you think you need to accomplish during this time.

You don't have to write a cookbook right now. Maybe you quietly cocoon yourself now and then later, in 2 months, the cookbook seems to write itself in a short time.

Let yourself move with the natural cycles of things.

There are also times of rest and going inward.

Caller 3:

Yes, thank you.

Rebecca:

Thank you.

Thinking vs Experiencing

Caller 4:

I think I feel the need to continue in the same direction as the two previous callers, and ask for some clarification.

I feel a little stupid asking this question.

Can you give an example of what is meant by "when things come up"?

Do you mean past memories, things you wish you hadn't done... is that the kind of thing you're saying is coming up? I know then we're supposed to sit and send love to them, but I don't know what you mean by "when things come up."

Rebecca:

It's the whole experience of life.

And it's not that you're "supposed to" sit and send love to them, it's about fully experiencing them, whatever that is.

It can be a past memory (like you said), or anything in your current experience which you react to or have discomfort or judgement about.

It can be thoughts which feel repetitive or disturbing to you. It can be whatever emotions you feel some judgement or resistance about, rather then allowing them to arise and fall away.

Caller 4:

So you're saying give in to that feeling of anger, or just noticing it? I just want it explained more.

Rebecca:

You think the explaining will lead to an understanding, but understanding comes from the experience.

So let's start with something you mentioned at first, that you felt stupid about asking the question. That's something that arose.

Let that idea and judgement about yourself come out into the open. Let yourself feel and experience it.

Let yourself experience what it feels like to judge yourself as stupid, or as less than in any way.

Bring out the question, "Does Love Love you anyway?"

It's always about a question and curiosity.

When you try to impose a new thing over an existing thing, then you're still in separation and duality where you make one right and one wrong.

That's why people run into trouble with the idea, "I'm not supposed to judge myself. I'm only supposed to love myself," which leads to more judgement about the judgement and continues to add more tension.

But that's not how Love works. Love is all-embracing and has no opposite.

Does Love still Love you, even if you're stupid, even if you're judging yourself, even if you're anything?

Caller 4:

Absolutely.

Rebecca:

Let yourself surrender into that.

Let Love start to carry you and guide you into what is changeless.

There's something in you, which is there before you judge yourself, remains the same while you judge yourself, and is still untouched after you've judged yourself and if you didn't judge yourself anymore.

Love will bring you there.

The more of your attention rests there, in the changeless, the easier it is for you to experience anything.

You mentioned anger. Invite up something you've felt angry or frustrated about.

Invite that into your attention now.

Invite any raw anger or frustration out into the open.

Give the anger permission to arise ...

to be experienced...

and then to return to where it came from.

You can follow it there.

What everything is looking to do is take us back home.

Everything you could possibly experience is your ride back home.

Most people just aren't getting on that bus. They expect it to look different than it does.

They see anger arise and think, "That's not it; that won't take me to peace."

But it is. Everything has the same source.

Caller 4:

I feel that, thank you.

Previously I had been trapped in that duality of trying to do what I thought I was supposed to do.

The question of wondering if Love Loves me helped a lot.

Rebecca:

It's not a mental exercise. And when we hand it off to the mind, it does it the way it's built to do things - it does it in duality and sorts things into two columns.

If you want to give the mind a task, give it one of curiosity.

Your mind can help insert a reminder in the form of a question, then something deeper in you brings you back home.

Do you feel that?

Caller 4:

Yes, I do. Thank you so much.

Rebecca:

Thank you for bringing it up.

Loving "Less Than"

Caller 5:

I keep bursting out in tears of relief. This whole call has been so healing and has been bringing me home. I'm so grateful.

What had been up for me was feelings of helplessness about an elder parent who lives alone far away, and I can't get there.

Rebecca:

What is your direct experience of that?

Caller 5:

It's dissipating now, but I was feeling guilt and not-enough-ness.

Rebecca:

Let's bring the "not enough," the "less than" out into the open.

Have a nice deep breath.

Step back and invite up what in the past seemed too painful to get close to.

Now let yourself go closer to that whole energy of not enough and less than.

Let curiosity come into play.

Let the question float out into the air, "Does Love already Love that?"

Does Love itself already Love everything in you that believes it's less than, everything in you that believes it's not enough?

Is all of it already Loved? Does it arise in Love from stillness and changelessness? Is it carried by Love until it returns to changelessness?

Check and see.

Caller 5:

Yes. It's unwinding now. I just feel space.

My muscles have been so tense; more than I had realized. But now they're relaxed and have let go of so much.

Rebecca:

Keep opening up and letting Love wash through everything.

Let Love wash through your physical body, through your thoughts, let Love soothe your mind.

Let Love open up the space for all your emotions to move freely and bring themselves back to source and back into harmony.

This lets you return home and lets your point of identification rest back in the Truth of you.

Let Love be the gateway for you.

Caller 5:

Thank you so much, Rebecca.

Rebecca:

You're welcome. Thank you.

Rebecca:

That's it.

Love is what everyone is yearning for, more than anything.

Even survival is second to the yearning for Love and the yearning to be in the Truth of who you Are, to remember who you really Are.

If someone feels completely separate from Love, they are willing to commit suicide because the pain of feeling separate from Love feels too great to bear, and survival takes a back seat.

Your strongest yearning is to consciously Be what you Are and to know your oneness with the Love you Are, and rest in that.

Maintaining Peace

Caller 6:

Right now I am "stranded in paradise."

I was on vacation with family, and my physicians advised me to stay here.

I had intuition to spend time with myself and not put any pressure on the family members who are here with me. I followed that intuition and I don't feel guilty about allowing myself to be on honeymoon with my own being-ness. But today things have arisen which I need to take care of, but I feel anger, dislike, frustration, and annoyance at the idea of interrupting my stillness to take care of anything.

Then I feel bad about myself for getting angry about any interruptions.

I just don't want to do anything - not even return a phone call. I just want to sit here and do nothing.

Rebecca:

That's separation coming into play.

What you described as a honeymoon with your own Being, when you are truly in that, nothing can interrupt it because it already contains everything.

And the Love which is part of it is already all-embracing.

Nothing can interrupt it because there's nothing outside of it.

So the anger you described isn't separate from the truth of your Being - it arises from it and it resolves within it.

Let's let the separation between what you feel is Peace and anger dissolve away.

Let the separation between what you feel is Peace and any frustration, resistance, anything you think could interrupt it, fall away.

There's nothing which isn't already contained within that Peace. There's nothing which doesn't have the same source. There's nothing which doesn't arise from the stillness within you. There's nothing which doesn't return to the stillness within you.

There's nothing that's not embraced by Love, and nothing can disturb what is changeless.

Let yourself notice all the separations that have been in place…

and give those separations permission to fall away.

Let them start to melt back down and dissolve.

The Peace of Being goes with you everywhere.

It's there with you when you return a phone call; it's with you when you don't return a phone call.

It's with you if you go out in the world and do things; it's with you if you stay inside sitting still.

The question is: are you looking toward it in any of those moments or are you looking away from it in any of those moments?

The easiest way to look toward it in any of those moments is to follow what arises from it back into it.

It's not about imposing a harsher and harsher separation in order to try to protect yourself or protect your peace from what you think the outside intrusions are.

The nature of Peace is that there are no outside intrusions to it.

Everything is within you and within that Peace.

Anything which seems to be the opposite of it is just a vehicle to take you deeper into it.

Caller 6:

Yes, thank you very much Rebecca.

Rebecca:

Thank you for bringing this up. You're Welcome.

Embracing Suppressed Feelings

Caller 7:

I've been implementing a morning practice from a previous course with you and it has been amazing.

I would love to work with you today. I'm feeling extremely safe and ok, but there is an underlying anxiety and fear of being uncomfortable with the awareness of being safe, if that makes any sense.

Rebecca:

Take a nice deep breath.

I understand your mind has ideas and questions about what you're feeling.

Let your mind know you acknowledge it, and you Love it, and this isn't its task - it doesn't have to be the one to solve this.

Caller 7:

Okay

Rebecca:

So now let the undercurrent of anxiety and fear you described come more out into the open.

Let it become more than an undercurrent.

Let it be your full experience now.

Let it have your whole attention.

Caller 7:

Ok, yeah

Rebecca:

Now follow it where it goes.

If you let it move freely, where does it go?

Let it be your vehicle that takes you back home.

Let yourself follow it back to its source…

which will also be your source…

which will be changeless stillness and Peace that contains all-embracing Love.

Caller 7:

Yeah, beautiful.

Rebecca:

Keep doing that; that's it.

Caller 7:

It's amazing. I'm smiling, my body's smiling.

I needed a nudge to give full permission for it to be out in the open. It's beautiful.

Rebecca:

What you did just now is all you ever have to do.

Caller 7:

Yeah, it really is the simplicity of that.

Rebecca:

And really it's even less than that. There's no doing required. There's just a little bit of doing at the beginning to remind you that you don't need to do.

Caller 7:

Yeah, I can give the mind space to be out of the way and fall into a place of curiosity.

I get what you're saying. I get it on a visceral level.

Beautiful, thank you.

Rebecca:

Thank you.

Resolving Your Biggest Fear

Caller 8:

During the call, I feel like a lot has been resolved already.

I feel pretty good. I started the call feeling like I wanted to put myself under my bed and never come out again, and now I feel like from this peaceful place, whatever happens doesn't really matter.

But the thing I'm left with is that I live in a crowded city and once I leave my home I have to touch so many things and come in contact with so many things. And even though my level of concern has decreased from what it was a few weeks ago, there's a lot of concern over the level of contact in the physical world outside my home.

Rebecca:

Let's back up, because you already gave yourself the answer - it doesn't really matter what happens. That's true, but what does matter is who you believe you are while it happens.

Let's look at your point of identification.

The same activities inside of or outside of your home can be done from different points of identification.

What happens when as you undertake those activities, your point of identification rests in Truth, in what is unchanged by any of those activities or their possible outcomes?

What happens when as you do those activities, your point of identification rests in stillness and the Peace and all-embracing Love it contains?

Caller 8:

That's definitely better.

I'm less concerned then about potentially bringing something home to my spouse, which is the biggest thing I've been carrying around.

If it was just me …

Rebecca:

You have the chance to notice what your biggest fear actually is in this situation.

It doesn't matter what it is. It doesn't matter if you think it matches what other people have or if it doesn't. It doesn't mean anything either way.

What's important is to invite that biggest fear, whatever it is, fully out into the open, without engaging with the mind explaining or comparing it to anything.

Invite the fear out into the open …

and let the fear be your vehicle back home.

Instead of trying to do anything to the fear - stop it, change it, manipulate it - just jump on and follow it where it goes.

Let it take you back to its source.

Where does the fear fall back into when you give it space and follow it?

Caller 8:

I feel defenseless.

Rebecca:

Follow the defenselessness, the helplessness, to its source.

What does it return to when it's complete?

What is unchanged before you feel helpless, during the feeling of helplessness, and after you no longer feel helpless? What remains untouched through all of it?

Let yourself and the helplessness and the fear be embrace by the Love which already does embrace it all.

Let that Love start to wash through you.

Open up.

When you're open, you're open and when you're closed, you're closed. When you were trying not to feel the fear, then it was also difficult for you to feel the Love that's coursing through your very Being in every moment.

But if you open up, to let yourself feel even the fear, now suddenly you can taste the Love too.

Caller 8:

Yeah, I feel that.

I feel better.

Rebecca:

And remember, it's not about going back into separation to try to maintain feeling better.

Let the process keep unfolding and let Love embrace everything.

Leave yourself open to letting everything arise and following it all to its source.

Let it all bring you back home into Love, Peace, Truth.

Then there's an infinitely expanding field of Love and Peace and everything beyond what we can describe in words.

Caller 8:

Yeah, I see that trying to make sense of it is a ridiculous, futile thing.

Rebecca:

The mind tries anyway, bless its heart.

Always give your mind permission to be embraced in Love.

Caller 8:

So when the mind picks up on ideas that bring up fear, just go with it? Just follow it back to source?

Rebecca:

Let your mind know you thank it for doing what it thinks it can to protect you. Let it be embraced in Love and rest there.

Then notice what is under the thoughts. What all the thoughts were trying to divert your attention from and prevent is the raw feeling underneath.

Invite up that raw feeling and give it your attention. Be present with it so it has the space to harmonize.

If your mind needs a task, the task is curiosity.

The mind can insert questions then just observe.

For example, "I wonder if Love already Loves this..." is a great exploration for the mind to use.

That's what the mind can do; the rest takes care of itself.

Caller 8:

Yeah, that's what I experienced. Thank you very much.

Rebecca: Thank you.

Experiencing Freedom

Caller 9:

After a caller, you talked about survival and that brought up a lot for me.

I'm ready to open up to my sovereignty in a way that I won't equate my value with money.

Rebecca:

The construct generally imposed on people *is* that their value is equated to money, and you're transmuting some of it in addition to what you're noticing in you.

Take a nice deep breath.

Let's take it as a whole then.

Go beyond your individual person and let your identification shift back into Truth, back into the All of you.

Get in touch with the raw energy of servitude which comes with taking beings and equating their worth to money, currency, exchange, and notice all the pain and untruth of it.

Let it arise.

Let it all be consumed by the Love you Are.

Let Love consume and transmute it.

Allow the opening up of freedom and liberation which comes from the dissolving of the pain and untruth.

Let that unfold.

Welcome the Truth and sovereignty which now arises and let it unfold.

There's a visual of chains falling, but as the chains fall, all the molecules of the chains turn into little butterflies which fly all around.

Do you feel that?

Caller 9:

(Laughing)

It's absolutely amazing what I've been feeling.

I didn't see that visual, but I totally felt it and I align with it. It's beautiful.

Rebecca:

That's a big wave of Love.

So what did you say in the beginning about survival?

Caller 9:

You said something earlier that Love is actually a bigger concern for us than survival, and something in it just hit me and I've been feeling something in me ever since you said that.

And as you took me through this, I could feel and see the world free and people free in what they truly are and it's so beautiful.

There's a feeling of falling back into Love and letting Love keep catching us. It felt so beautiful and I was feeling it for me and everyone. Thank you.

Rebecca:

Thank you.

CONCLUSION

Rebecca:

Take a nice deep breath everyone.

Many people are wrapped up right now in survival, even though Love is the ultimate yearning.

Give permission for every being to start to become aware of the Love they are already embraced by.

Love is already there. Love is already burning inside everyone. It is already surrounding and embracing every person.

But there's an opening which happens and then someone notices the Love is there and then allows it to saturate them.

Let this cascade happen. Let this chain reaction be set off - of these little openings that become big openings, that become full-blown unfoldings and bloomings in Love… from Love… through Love.

Stay with the simplicity of that.

Let everything be the vehicle deeper into it.

It's so simple, and everything takes you there if you let it.

Everything takes you back to the Truth if you let it.

Set aside all your ideas and beliefs you're invested in about your identity, about anyone else's identity, all of it.

Don't invest attention and ideas and belief into anything.

Just let everything return you to your own Love.

Give your attention to your own Love and Peace, and keep letting everything bring you there.

There's no system of ideas or beliefs, no system of anything, that can't collapse.

But what always remains is You.

What always remains is the still, changeless, Peace and Love you Are.

I invite everyone to put your attention there now and always.

Let it be your whole focus.

And when I say let it be your whole focus, it can always be your whole focus.

It can be your whole focus while you brush your teeth, while you take a shower, while you make a meal…

while you sit and don't do anything else.

It's not the external movement or stillness that determines the true stillness.

When you tap deep enough into the true stillness, the external can move and move and move, and it makes no difference to your stillness.

When you're not tapped into the true stillness, the external can sit until it rots, and you still won't feel still.

Have another nice deep, gentle breath.

Give permission for every single cell in your body to just fall backwards into Love, to open and relax into the all-embracing Love with no opposite.

Relax into the Love that just Is.

Surrender to the Love which even as it is sought after and yearned for, is always there underneath all the yearning, all the seeking.

The yearning itself is already all you need to take you home. But what gets layered on top of it is all the machinations of the mind of about how to solve the yearning, and what to do about the yearning.

If you would just feel the yearning itself, if you would follow it, it will take you back home.

It has always been designed to return you to the Love you Are.

The yearning arises from the the stillness, the changeless Peace and Love, and it returns to the stillness, the changeless Peace and Love.

So feel the yearning; experience it directly, and follow it back home.

Follow it back into who and what you truly Are.

Then stay there. Remain there.

Remain there not by blocking anything out or trying to separate from anything, but by letting your identification rest in what it has always rested in, what it always has been and always will be.

Remain in what no one can give you and no one can take away.

No one can fix you or save you -

and that's good news because it also means no one can destroy you.

It's you. It's always you and it always has been you.

Because you Are Love and Love is All there is.

You Are Love and Love is All there is.

Thank you for being here, for being you, for Being.

ADDITIONAL
EXPLORATIONS

Exploration 1

Begin With Truth

Take a few moments to settle in.

Start to give your full attention to the movement of your breath.

Make sure you've set aside this time and your attention to be present with yourself, to go inward, to be open and receive.

Come into this space without expectation, or agenda, or judgement.

Let yourself be open to something more than your mind already knows how to understand.

Come into this space with the knowing that you already are more than enough, rather than coming into this space to fix yourself or add something to you that you think you're missing.

Come into this space to remember and reconnect with more and more of the totality of what you really Are.

Anything and everything you seem to receive is really just your awareness opening up to what you already Are.

Take a few more slow, deep, gentle breaths as you allow yourself to settle into those intentions.

Now bring your attention right into the center of yourself.

Let yourself become aware of the changeless in you.

Throughout all of your experience, all of what you've considered the best and worst moments, the most forgettable moments, what has remained unchanged through all of those?

Let that start to have more of your attention now.

The answer to everything is Truth, and Truth is changeless.

One of the easiest ways to connect with the Truth of yourSelf, without any preconceived ideas about what it is, without any agenda or expectation, is to connect with what in you has never changed and doesn't ever change.

The changeless will reveal to you what it contains, which is Peace, Love, Joy.

But oftentimes if you're trying to connect with Peace, Love, or Joy, you may be approaching it with an agenda.

There's so much misunderstanding of what Love even is.

If your perception of Love is skewed and you focus yourself on what you think it is, then that distortion becomes amplified.

So go for Truth first.

Then you'll find in the Truth that you already hold infinite Love for yourself, you already are the source of infinite Love, you are the expression of infinite Love.

The most important thing you can do is to remember who and what you really Are.

The knowing of yourself resolves everything else.

When you begin from misunderstanding of what you are, there is easily a belief that you need to be fixed or improved, because who you are is somehow faulty.

Everything you do from that perspective just perpetuates itself.

But if you start from placing a priority on Truth, then the rest will fall into place.

Always begin from Truth.

There's nothing you need to add to yourself.

Exploration 2

Integrating the Mind

Take a moment to settle in.

Give yourself the space to be open to everything available to you - everything that has always been available to you.

Nice deep breath.

Give your body permission to relax.

Allow it to receive all that's brought with the breath.

Let your mind bring you whatever it's concerned about.

Also let your mind bring you everything you've been striving for, searching for, trying to be, trying to achieve, trying to improve - that whole list it has of all those things it thinks it needs to be doing for you, that it thinks it needs to be adding to you, that it thinks it needs to be finding for you.

Invite all of it out into the open.

Give it the opportunity to come up all at once so you can be completely present with all of it.

Look at what your mind has been working so hard about because of what it thinks you aren't enough of or you don't have enough of.

Invite up everything your mind thinks you need more of…

and also everything it thinks you need less of.

Invite up whatever you think are your flaws or bad habits or problems...

everything you mind has been working so hard to remove from you.

Let that all show up - everything you've been trying to add to or remove from yourself, until your poor mind doesn't even know which way is up.

It's been running back and forth - "I need a little more of this, a little less of this..." "almost, almost, almost, and pretty soon I'll have it right."

Let yourself see all of that now for exactly what it is.

What if you invite your mind to take a moment to sit here with you, to be in a place of Love, and to start to just observe what's actually here?

Start to observe who and what you actually Are.

Nice deep breath.

Let the Truth of yourself bubble up into your attention.

Let your mind start to see that its job is not what it thought it was.

Let it see that you naturally have nothing which needs to be added or removed.

The mind has so much pressure on it now when it believes all these modifications it's trying to make are related to you at your very core, at your very identity.

That's why it's so life-and-death to the mind, because whatever it thinks it needs to add or remove is going to make you what you are, which will pass the test or not.

But that's not true.

Then the mind hears things about how you are whole, complete, and perfect already, and it interprets that as meaning nothing will never change or grow or expand.

And that's not true either.

Who you Are is unshakeable, and needs nothing added and nothing removed.

Your mind will notice the process of your Truth aligning and shifting your external experience and you start to embody Truth.

It's not the either-or the mind has been seeing it as.

It's not: either you're a fundamentally flawed thing which needs fixing OR because you're already perfect nothing has the capacity to change.

Who you Are is already more than all that your mind has been trying to gather for you.

Your expression of it, your embodiment of it, may or may not be yet.

This recognition changes your mind's path completely.

It still has a task, but it's not at all interwoven with your identity, with your worth, with who and what you fundamentally Are.

Let relief take hold in your mind as it recognizes the stakes aren't what it thought they were for its part in this.

Nice deep breath.

Check in with all the things the mind thinks need to be fixed and changed, added and removed, accomplished and achieved.

What if rather than working outside-in, where the mind is charged with arranging all of that until it's all perfect so that can make you what you are (which is a daunting task indeed) … what if instead the mind sees the Truth of it, which is the other way around.

The totality of who and what you are, which already is more than everything the mind could hope to get you to be … is moving out through the mind and the mind is only in charge of moving and gathering in a way which aligns with that.

The mind gets into cooperation with what you already Are, so externally there can be shifts and changes as that begins showing up in alignment with what you already Are.

Everything can show up as an expression, an embodiment of what you already Are.

The mind has been caught in the middle with the whole thing backwards.

It has thought it needs to bring things in from outside to make you what you are, instead of allowing what you Are to express and embody itself out.

Another deep breath.

Let all this start to settle.

Exploration 3

The Changeless

Take a minute to settle in.

Take a few moments in quiet and allow yourself to set aside this time and attention for yourself.

Be willing to give yourself the gift of your own presence.

Be willing to be open to receive beyond what your mind could expect, anticipate, or even understand.

Bring more attention to following your breath as it moves through your system.

Give your body permission to relax into receiving all that's brought with your breath.

Give your attention permission to settle into what in you is changeless.

Let the changeless have more of your attention.

Bring more of your conscious awareness to what in you is untouched by anything.

Bring more attention to what in you remains the same whether you are angry or elated, that remains the same through every moment you felt disappointed as well as every moment you thought you got your way.

What is it that's been unchanged by any experience?

Let that have more of your attention now.

Rather than spending lifetimes of effort to try to get all of your experiences to fall on one side of duality, what if you give more of your attention to what is untouched by anything?

It embraces all.

There's no separation.

When more of your attention is with the changeless, that opens the space for you to fully experience everything for the first time.

Otherwise, even every "good" experience is hampered and resisted because it already contains the seed of its opposite.

With more of your attention resting in the changeless, start to open more and give attention to what has been waiting for your attention.

Notice what has lined up because it needs your Love and attention for resolution.

Welcome everything that's been pushed aside, looked away from, ignored, rejected, judged.

Have a nice deep breath.

Extend the invitation to all the things which had previously been rejected, which you felt you couldn't experience or you didn't want to experience.

Let them all come into your attention now.

See what it's like to give yourself permission to fully experience them now, from the perspective of the changeless.

You've previously resisted experiencing these things because of the belief that you're subject to them.

But what if you aren't?

What if you can let more of your attention and more of your identity rest in the Truth of you, so you feel free to allow all experiences?

For example, what about the experience of feeling powerless?

Your willingness to embrace and allow that experience of feeling powerless and let your identification rest in the changeless, opens up your experience and embodiment of your own sovereignty.

Another experience you might resist is loss.

Invite into your attention the feeling of loss, or the anticipation of loss, the expectation of devastation and pain.

Let that flood into your awareness and let yourself experience it exactly as it is.

Give it your full attention.

Allow it to be as intense as it is.

Find out what it's like to just experience it.

A helpful practice is to always start from Truth.

If you find yourself resisting an experience or resisting a feeling coming through your attention, there's no need to employ your favorite manipulations to make it go away or try to make yourself feel better because you think you're not supposed to experience it.

Doing that always leaves you with the residue of its opposite.

Then there's an undercurrent of expectation that at some point, your manipulation, your tool or trick, might not work.

All the while, you believe the feeling is something you can't or shouldn't experience, which is always a lie.

Starting from the Truth means that when you find yourself resisting something or having an experience you don't like, instead of trying to change it, ask "What Am I?"

Even if you only have an intellectual starting point of belief because you've heard that you are not a limited being which that feeling or experience is too much for, use that as your starting point.

Then test it out.

Don't try to dissolve a feeling because you think you don't want to experience it.

That leaves you in the same cycle over and over again.

Instead, ask yourself, "Is it true that I have to resist this feeling?" Start from there.

Have a nice deep breath.

Let yourself be rooted in whatever you can perceive in this moment as the greatest Truth of what you Are.

From there, invite into your attention what you previously misbelieved was too much for you to experience, too painful for you to experience.

Let it come flooding through your awareness.

The height of Love allows everything and is all-embracing.

It's not about an intense feeling of a favorite.

It's wide open and aligns itself with the Truth of your Being.

Keep allowing all-embracing Love to embrace all you experience.

Exploration 4

Awareness

Take a few minutes to settle in.

Take a moment to make sure you've set aside this time and attention for yourself.

Give yourself your full attention.

Be open to receive all that's available to you, beyond what your mind already knows how to understand.

Give yourself the space to really dive into what it's like to spend this time in a space of complete Love.

Allow yourself the ease and relaxation and nourishment that comes with being completely immersed in the recognition of the Love that you Are.

To do that, begin by having some deep, gentle breaths.

Allow your breath to be as slow as it can.

Give your body the opportunity to receive all that's brought with the breath.

Allow your mind to settle into being able to just observe.

Give the mind the opportunity to just notice, to just meet what comes to your attention.

Let your mind just observe your breath and observe your body, to observe the thoughts that pass through, to observe the energy and feelings and emotions that arise.

Let yourself notice what happens as you allow this greater and greater awareness to be present.

Notice how different that is than just a string of ideas or a string of judgements.

Give yourself the space to just observe everything that arises, without the idea of what it should or shouldn't be, without the idea you need to fix it or change it or alter it or improve it in any way.

See what you're able to notice in your body, exactly as it is.

See what you're able to notice as a sensation without ideas about what it should be.

See what you're able to notice about your thoughts, even if some of those thoughts are judgments or ideas about how things should be.

See what it's like to step back and not add that layer of investment and engagement by then having ideas about whether those thoughts and judgements should be there or not.

So even when there's a judgement or an idea, just give it permission to be as it is.

What if you just being aware of it is already enough?

That's foreign to the mind.

But what if awareness is already enough?

And what if you turn that same attention to the emotions, the feelings, the energy, you notice arising and moving through your system, that you may notice yourself braced against or trying to hold back, trying to manage or control…

What if it's already enough to notice them?

What if your awareness of them is exactly what they need from you, without all the additional layers of ideas about what should or shouldn't be, and why they're good or bad or right or wrong?

See what it's like, notice what arises in you, when you allow yourself to just meet them, to just be with them exactly as they are.

Let yourself relax even more.

Start to pay attention to letting your breath move into your heart.

With each breath, let it move deeper and deeper into the center of your heart, however you experience that.

Give your whole system permission to relax into the waves of deeper and deeper Love, that embrace you exactly as you are…

The Love that knows no bounds and has no opposite.

The Love that is all-embracing and all-encompassing.

The Love that has no conditions and no limits.

Allow yourself to dive deeper and deeper into that Love now.

Take three nice deep breaths all the way through your whole body.

Exploration 5

Does Love Love This?

Take a few minutes to settle in.

Make sure you have this time set aside for yourself.

Feel free to give yourself your full attention.

Start by bringing your breath deeply and gently through your whole body for a few minutes.

Give that your whole attention.

Let your whole occupation be to watch what it's like for your breath to move into your body, to watch your breath circulate in your body, deliver all that it delivers, and watch it move back out.

Allow yourself to begin to notice the ease in that.

Give yourself permission to open up; and allow yourself to receive fully all that's brought with your breath.

Let yourself receive all that's available now, even more than what your mind could've thought to expect or anticipate, and even beyond what the mind knows how to understand.

Let yourself receive beyond your mind's understanding, beyond your mind's expectation.

Check in and see if you're willing now to open up more of your conscious awareness to the Love that's already present.

With a light curiosity, see what it's like to just notice the Love that's already there.

Let yourself perceive it in whatever way is natural to you.

Start to notice the Love that's already present in what seems to be the inside of you.

Allow yourself to become more aware of it.

Let more of it have your attention.

Let more of the Love which seems to be external to you, which seems to be surrounding you, start to light up in your awareness.

Start to notice more of the Love you're immersed in right now.

It's not something you have to generate, or get from anywhere or anyone.

Don't depend upon your mind (or try to coerce your mind) to be something which generates boundless, unconditional, Love with no opposite. The mind isn't built for that.

Let your mind off the hook and give it permission to not understand true Love, while allowing it to be Loved anyway.

Bring into your attention all the time you've spent trying to get your mind or your constructed personality to get on board with doing what it thinks is Love.

If you have to get it on board, that's done from a place of separation and duality, where it could just as easily do the opposite.

But the Love I'm referring to has no opposite, so it's not something your mind, your constructed personality, your ego, really understands at all.

Love can seem to be newly experienced, but Love already exists. It's always present.

Although Love can move through your mind and your ego to be experienced, it's not your mind generating it or your ego creating it.

Let go of the expectation for your mind or ego to become all Loving, because they don't even understand the truth of Love.

What is available to you instead, is to become more and more aware of, and accepting of, the boundless Love without opposite which is already present.

The more you become aware of, accepting of, and open to, allowing Love to come through your constructed self, then the more you experience Love.

It's not something you have to depend upon your mind or ego to generate.

Let yourself have three nice deep breaths into that.

See what it's like if you decide you're willing to be aware of Love, to allow Love, even while your mind may have judgements about things.

Of course your mind has judgements about things, that's how it's built.

Set your mind free to have all of its judgments and opinions.

None of that has to get in the way of Love.

None of it can prevent Love, not really.

Love is already there.

What matters is where your awareness and attention are placed.

I invite you to start to cultivate letting your attention be on Truth even in the midst of experiences which you have judgements against.

You believe that certain feelings can separate you from Love. That's why you don't like to feel certain things.

That's why you don't like to feel disappointed or angry or sad. Your resistance is all rooted in the belief that any of those feelings can separate you from Love.

You believe you can only have one or the other - that you can have any of those or you can have Love, and that those keep you from Love.

So then you reject so many of your feelings, but the reason they feel so uncomfortable to you is because you reject them.

In the act of rejecting them, because you think they separate you from Love, now you are turning away from Love.

You're not allowing Love through into your attention in that moment, and that's the real discomfort.

But Love is there all the time, whether you're aware of it or not.

Take another nice deep breath.

Let's dive further into this Love.

Invite into your attention something you tend to avoid, whether it's something you are currently rejecting or something you habitually don't like to experience.

With a light curiosity, ask yourself, "I wonder if Love already Loves this…"

Just notice what happens…

It's not about answering yes or no.

Just see what happens when you place your attention on wondering, "Does Love already Love this?"

That question gives the opportunity for Love that's already present to come into your awareness.

It gives the opportunity for you to put your attention on the Love that's already present.

You don't need the gymnastics of trying to get your mind (which doesn't even know how to Love) to Love things in order for you to have an experience of Love.

You can always experience Love. You can experience Love in the midst of your mind thinking whatever it thinks.

Have another nice deep breath.

See if you're willing to open up even more, even deeper, to allow the Love that's already present to flood into your attention, for you to be more aware of its presence, for you to be willing to accept more of its presence.

Whatever shows up in your experience, just ask: "I wonder if Love already Loves this…"

Take a nice deep breath and watch your breath move through your whole system.

Notice whatever comes into your attention in this moment.

Open up your curiosity and ask, "I wonder if Love already Loves this..."

Whatever comes into your attention: a thought, a feeling, the chair you're sitting on, the wall you see in front of you... whatever you notice, just ask, "I wonder if Love Loves this..."

The person who did you wrong one time...

the situation which feels challenging or insurmountable right now...

your memory of your whole life...

your idea of how close you've gotten to what you think is enlightenment...

Whatever arises, bring it into your attention.

With an open curiosity, ask, "I wonder if Love already Loves this..."

...and just notice what starts to happen.

Notice what starts to happen when you genuinely allow; with no agenda or expectation about what is the right or wrong answer, or the right or wrong experience...

Just enter into it for the pure curiosity of it ... "I wonder if Love already Loves this..."

I wonder if Love already Loves this...

If it seems there is no answer and nothing is happening -

or if there's just a bit more space, even if almost imperceptible, which starts to come into your attention -

or maybe right away you feel the Love that's already present flooding into your attention -

none of these experiences are right or wrong.

What's most important is your willingness to continue with the pure curiosity, which wonders, without agenda or expectation, "I wonder if Love already Loves this…"

You can wonder if Love already Loves you.

You can wonder if Love already Loves your mind, your body, your whole life situation, your whole world.

Just wonder…

"I wonder if Love already Loves this…"

Exploration 6

What is the Truth of This?

Take a few nice deep breaths.

Take a few minutes to gently give your attention to your breath.

Without trying to force your breath to do anything in particular, just let yourself yield to your breath as it moves through your whole system.

Give permission for your whole body to relax and open fully, to receive all that's brought with your breath.

Let your attention follow your breath, and notice the interaction between your body and your breath.

Go with your breath everywhere it goes.

Give your attention to whatever you find where your breath goes.

Anywhere there's restriction, bring your attention there so it can open up.

As you do that, let yourself also notice the feeling of the inside of your body as you follow your breath.

Let yourself notice what your whole body feels like from the inside.

Notice the sensation of having your attention inside your body.

Allow your attention to spread through the entire inside of your body.

Let your awareness wash through your whole body, then bring your attention to the center of your heart.

Notice what it's like to be aware of your existence from the center of your heart.

Now invite into this space anything that needs your attention - starting with anything which needs resolution, or your mind thinks needs to be fixed or changed, or undone, or improved.

Invite that into the center of this stillness at the center of your attention.

Find out what it's like to just be with it, exactly as it is.

Find out what it's like to meet it without expectation or judgement, without any preconceptions about what it is or what you think it needs to be.

Notice that up until now you've had a defined idea about it.

See what it's like to now meet it in this moment with only a pure curiosity, as if you've never known it before.

Let yourself meet it with no ideas about whether it's good or bad, without any expectations about what needs to happen to it, to fix it or change it.

Have curiosity to meet it now and really know it intimately and experience it (whatever you thought was wrong, whatever you thought needed improvement), exactly as it actually is.

Once you're willing to be fully present with it in that way, it now has the opportunity for the first time, to reveal to you what it was actually bringing.

Now there's space for you to respond to the invitation it has been bringing all along - an invitation deeper into Truth.

In your interactions up until now with _____ (whatever you're working with now), what have you wanted to avoid experiencing?

What have you not wanted to experience?

Go to the root of it.

Whatever you've been wanting to fix or change, the reason you've wanted to fix or change it is so you wouldn't have to experience something ... what is that something you don't want to experience?

The feeling, the energy, that you didn't want to experience; let it get your attention now.

What feeling or energy did you believe changing your circumstance or situation was going to liberate you from having to experience?

Whatever that feeling or energy is, allow yourself to now move toward it in a new way.

Give it your attention with a curiosity, with a willingness to meet it and experience it, exactly as it is.

If it's sadness, frustration, fear, insecurity, helplessness, powerlessness, anger...

Go toward it now with open curiosity.

Find out what it's like to just experience it, exactly as it is.

Give the feeling or energy plenty of space and an open embrace from you, to come freely through your awareness without being stifled or suppressed or rejected.

Now let's go deeper.

Check and see what you believed experiencing the feeling or energy you were avoiding experiencing would mean about you.

What did you think it was going to mean about your identity if you experienced what you were avoiding?

How were you afraid that experience was going to somehow change who you are, or who you think you would like to be?

Give yourself permission now to fully be or not be that identity.

For example, if the feeling you were avoiding was going to mean that your identity is now that you are a failure or less than, then give yourself permission to fully experience now in this moment that identity of failure or less than.

This question of identity is always at the root of all that you avoid.

There are so many identities you expend energy trying to acquire, trying to build and maintain, or trying to avoid and prevent.

So let all the tension of that work fall away.

Allow yourself to experience whatever is present.

What if you didn't have to avoid or reject that identity?

Your connection with Truth allows you to be free of the need to avoid, reject, pursue, or maintain any particular identity.

Set yourself free to experience any identity fully in this moment.

It doesn't mean you'll be stuck with whatever you allow yourself to experience now.

Instead, you will be free from using energy to reject it.

So regarding what was your uncomfortable experience, now ask "What it the Truth of this?"

Just let that question percolate.

You don't need to have an immediate answer or an answer in words.

The question itself will pull you into the experience of Truth, when you ask it with real curiosity.

Ask again, "What is the Truth of this?"

You can ask about the feeling, the identity, or even the original situation which started this inquiry for you.

Continue asking, "What is the Truth of this?" and allow yourself to receive and experience whatever arises for you.

Now you start to have a window to get back in touch with what it is in you that is changeless.

Allow the changeless in you to bubble up and have more and more of your attention.

Notice what it is in you that's unaffected by any experience, by any identity.

Notice what cannot be diminished or increased.

Allow more of your attention to go to that now.

You don't have to exclude anything to give the changeless your attention.

Because the Truth of you is unchanged by anything, you don't have to exert some mental effort to create a separation and focus "only" on the changeless.

The Truth of you already includes everything you could ever possibly experience, so if it seems something comes along looking for your attention, invite it in.

With your attention in the changeless, invite whatever arises into the center of the changelessness with you.

Notice what happens.

There's no separation. There's no either-or.

That's why there's no ultimate finish line for you to cross.

You don't need to be on a quest to reach some point where you think you won't experience anything anymore.

All along, your experience was never the problem, your rejection of it was.

What matters is not what happens in your experience, but who you think you are while it's happening.

The difficulty is in clinging to certain identities, reaching for certain identities, rejecting certain identities, all with the sense that those identities are what is real.

What liberates you, is a recognition of what you truly Are, so the comings and goings of any of those identities becomes insignificant to you.

They don't have to be gone, but you recognize them for what they are.

The first step is giving your presence, with openness and curiosity.

Your willingness to be fully present with anything and everything then starts to transform your experience of everything.

You'll notice things harmonizing themselves.

But that is really only the starting point.

Giving space for things to harmonize just eases your way to allow you to put more and more attention on the Truth of yourself, until you discover that what you Are *is* that space, and everything it contains.

You Are the presence, the Love, the awareness you thought you were bringing to things or surrendering to.

Once that takes place, it opens another door for the full expression of what you're here to embody to flow through you.

There was no space for that when you were clinging to having certain identities and rejecting certain identities.

Then, the more you are identified with Truth, the less you are dependent upon any outcomes or whether your mind calls them good or bad.

The real gift available to you, which you're trying to beckon yourself into, is being completely not dependent upon anything being what the mind calls good.

Take a moment now to dive into that.

Let yourself experience what it's like to not feel limited by any particular outcome.

Take a deep breath and drop further into that.

Notice what is actually available to you when you are no longer dependent upon "goodness" for your peace and happiness.

When you are no longer bound by death or loss, or by the fear of those, what is available to you?

What if what you Are is something other than anything you ever thought you were?

What if it's other than even the best, most perfect idea of what you hope you could be?

If you can put a word on it, what you Are is more than that.

What if what you Are is something other than anything you ever thought you were or anything you could ever think you could be?

What you Are can't be named or limited by thought or expectation.

That's what I'm inviting you to give attention to, allow to flow through your whole experience, inform your whole life, and allow yourself to be a conduit of into the world.

Let yourself have three really nice, gentle, slow breaths.

Let yourself notice what's circulating through your attention now.

You can continue to explore with these questions:

1. What am I trying to avoid experiencing?

2. What do I think it means about me?

3. What is the Truth of this?

ABOUT REBECCA QUAVE

Rebecca is a catalyst of transformation and expansion of consciousness. She guides and supports you in unraveling exactly what's in the way of embodying and expressing the expansive love and unlimited potential you truly are.

Her natural gift of activating you to your highest truth creates profound shifts quickly and easily.

Because of her loving and surrendered nature which embraces you and your personal journey exactly as you are while supporting and guiding your unique process, some describe Rebecca as a midwife of spiritual expansion.

You can visit Rebecca at www.RebeccaQuave.com

If you found this material helpful, you can receive additional reminders from Rebecca by enrolling at:
www.RebeccaQuave.com/email

Other books from Rebecca are available at:
www.RebeccaQuave.com/books

www.ingramcontent.com/pod-product-compliance
Lightning Source LLC
LaVergne TN
LVHW011202080426
835508LV00007B/552